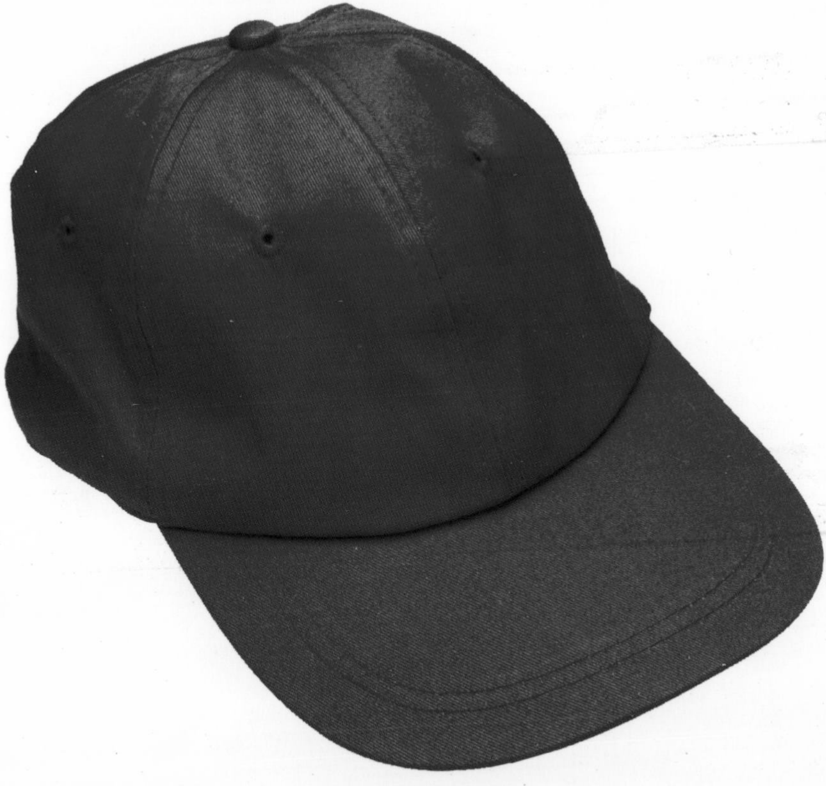

The cap is blue.

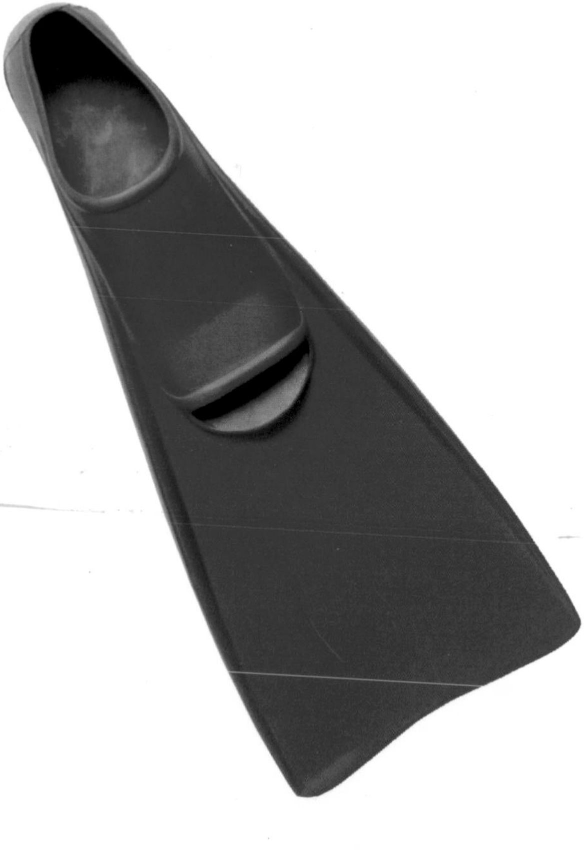

The fin is blue.

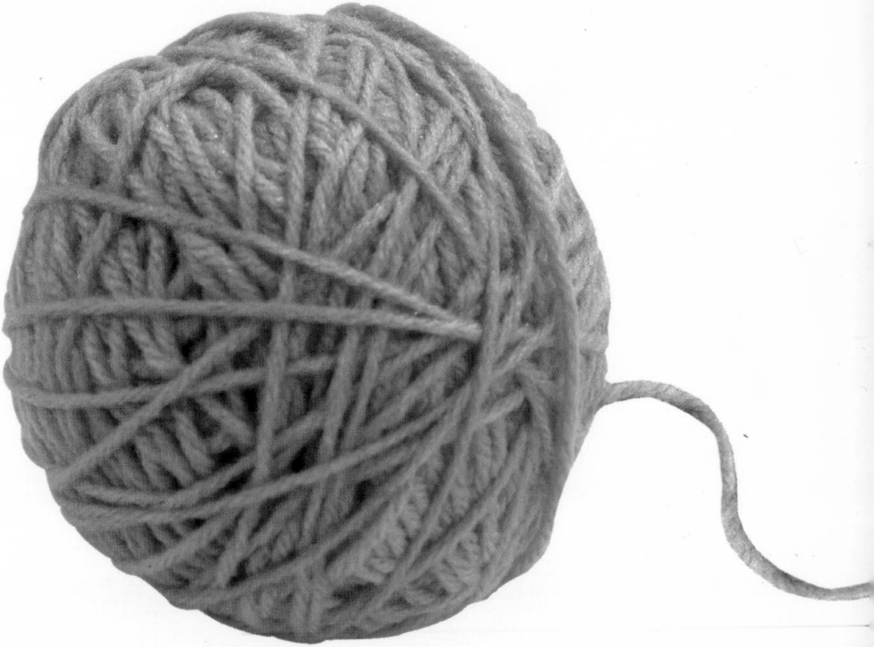

The yarn is blue.

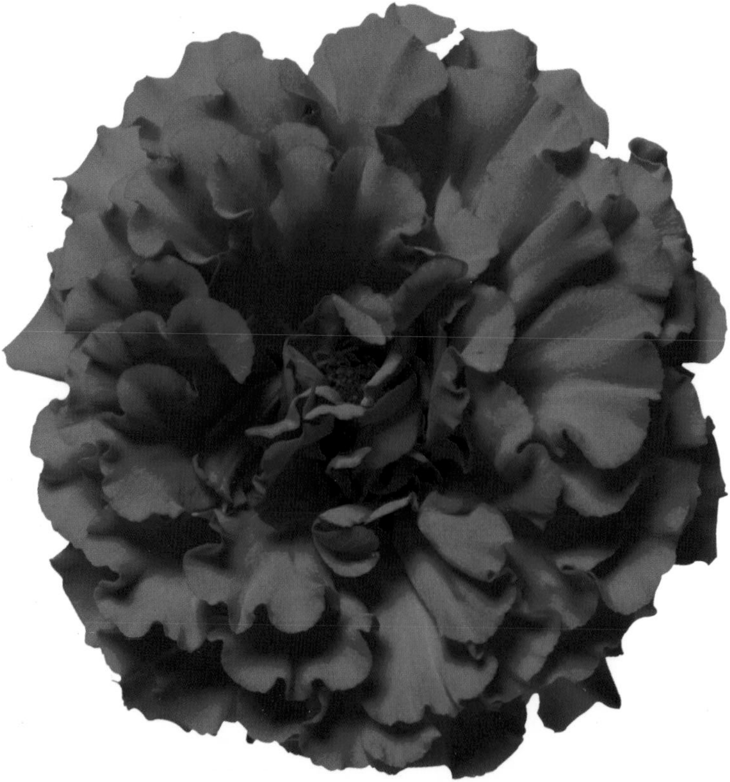

The flower is blue.

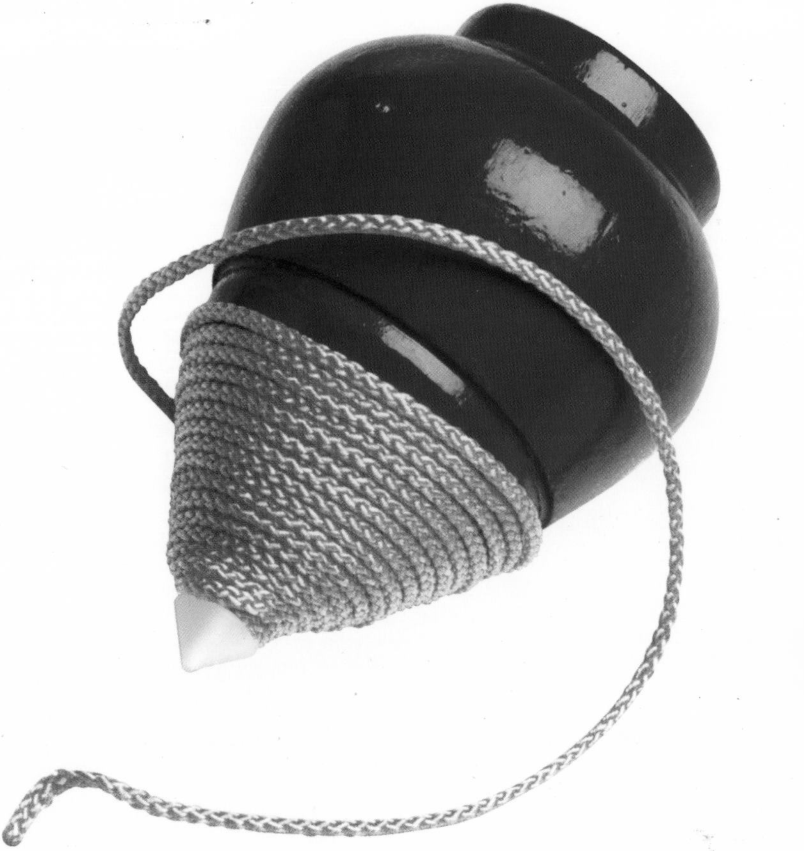

The top is blue.

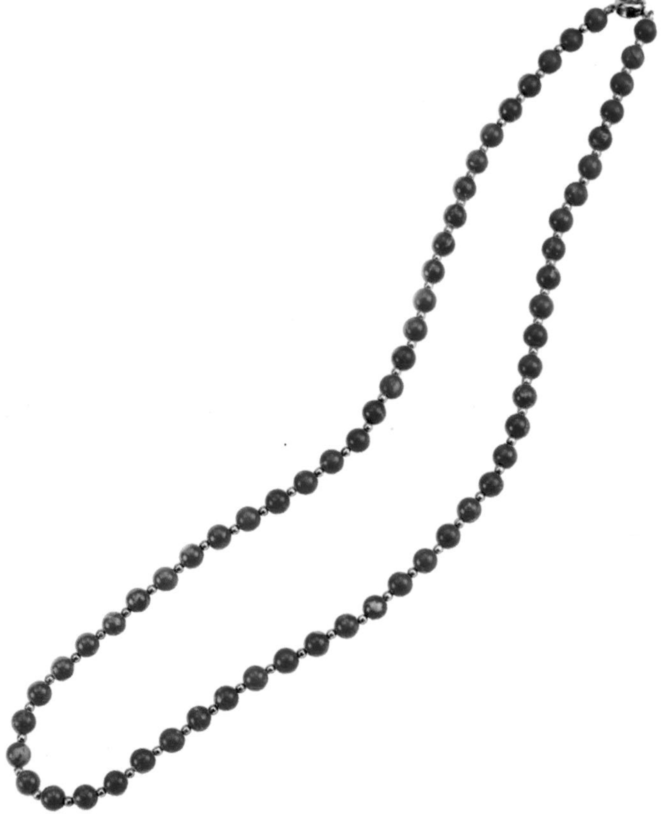

The necklace is blue.

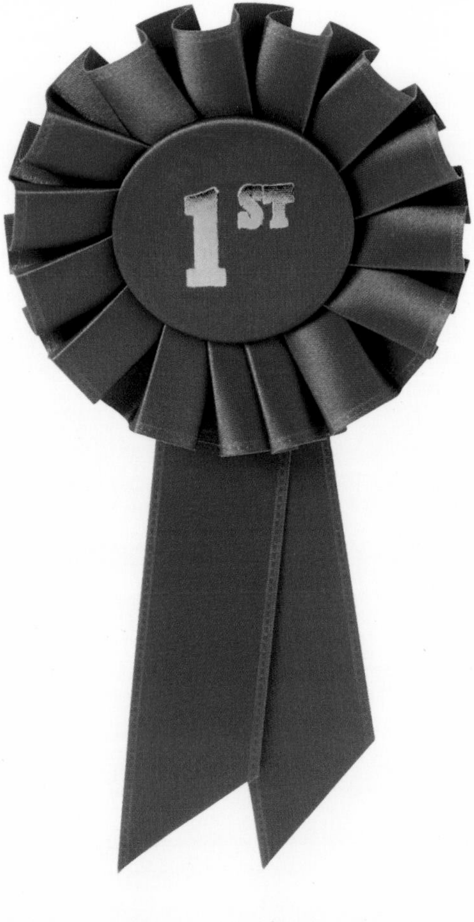

The ribbon is blue.

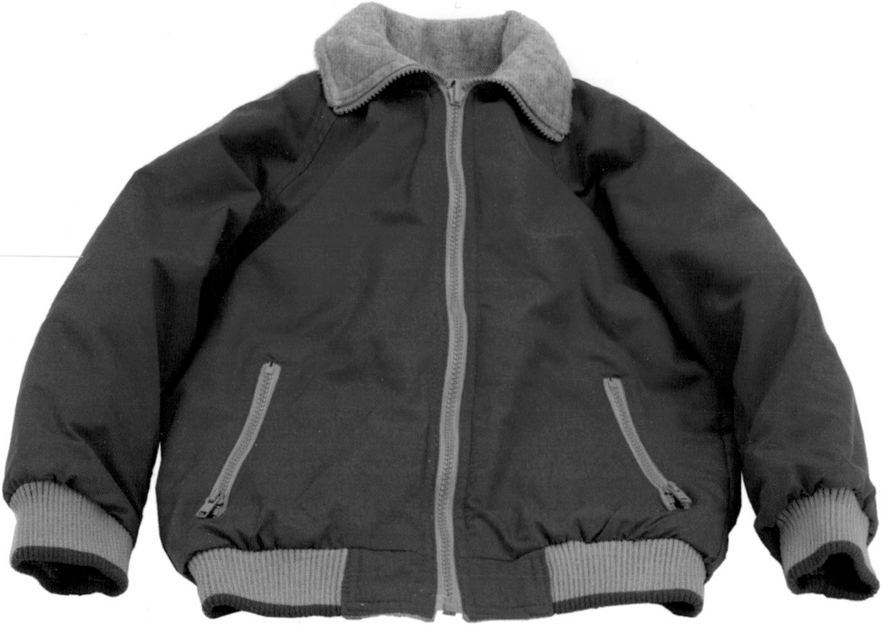

The jacket is blue.